Broadway Divas

Sing Along with 8 Great-Soun͡

C000044699

Contents

Alfred Publishing Co., Inc.
16320 Roscoe Blvd., Suite 100
P.O. Box 10003
Van Nuys, CA 91410-0003
alfred.com

ISBN-10: 0-7390-4445-1 (Book and CD)
ISBN-13: 978-0-7390-4445-2 (Book and CD)

Cover Art:
Broadway scene: © Corbis
Microphone: © istockphoto.com/Doctor_Bass

And All That Jazz

From *Chicago*
Lyrics by
FRED EBB
Music by
JOHN KANDER

Verse 1:
Come on, babe, why don't we paint the town,
and all that jazz!
I'm gonna rouge my knees
and roll my stockings down,
and all that jazz!
Start the car; I know a whoopee spot
where the gin is cold,
but the piano's hot.
It's just a noisy hall
where there's a nightly brawl,
and all that jazz!

Verse 2:
Oh, slick your hair and wear your buckle shoes,
and all that jazz!
I hear that Father Dip is gonna blow the blues,
and all that jazz!
Hold on, hon; we're gonna bunny hug.
I bought some aspirin down at United Drug
in case we shake apart
and want a brand-new start
to do that jazz!

Verse 3:
*(Oh, you're gonna see your Sheba shimmy shake,)
oh, and all that jazz!
(Oh, she's gonna shimmy till her garters break,)
oh, and all that jazz!
(Show her where to park her girdle.
Oh, her mother's blood'd curdle
if she'd hear her baby's queer for)
all that jazz!

Verse 4:
Find a flask; we're playin' fast and loose,
and and all that jazz!
(And all that jazz!)
Right up here is where I store the juice,
and all that jazz!
(And and all that jazz!)
Come on, babe, we're gonna brush the sky;
I betcha I betcha Lucky Lindy never flew so high.
'Cause in the stratosphere,
how could he lend an ear to.
all that *jazz!*

Spoken:
So that's final, huh, Fred?
(Fred: *Yeah, I'm afraid so, kiddo…*)
Oh, Fred…
(Fred: *Yeah?*)
Nobody walks out on me!

Outro:
No, I'm no one's wife,
but oh, I love my life
and all that jazz!
That jazz!

*Lyrics in parentheses indicate background vocals.

And All That Jazz

From *Chicago*

Lyrics by
FRED EBB

Music by
JOHN KANDER

Moderately ♩ = 116

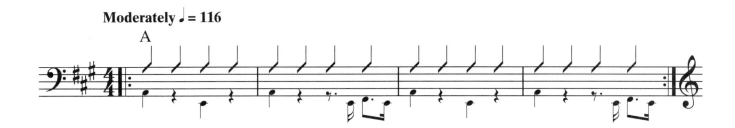

Verses 1 & 2:

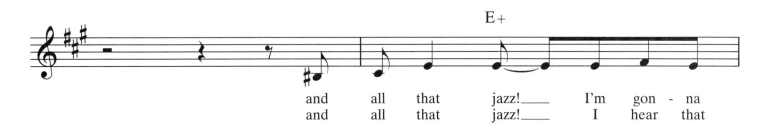

1. Come on, babe, why don't we paint the town,___
(2.) slick your hair___ and wear your buck - le shoes,___

and all that jazz!___ I'm gon - na
and all that jazz!___ I hear that

rouge my knees___ and roll my stock - ings down,___
Fa - ther Dip___ is gon - na blow the blues,___

and all that jazz!___ Start the car; I know a
and all that jazz!___ Hold on, hon;___ we're gon - na

And All That Jazz - 5 - 1
26499

4

whoop - ee spot___ where the gin is cold,___ but the pi -
bun - ny hug.___ I bought some as - pir - in___ down at U -

an - o's hot.___ It's just a nois - y hall___ where there's a
nit - ed Drug___ in case we shake a - part___ and want a

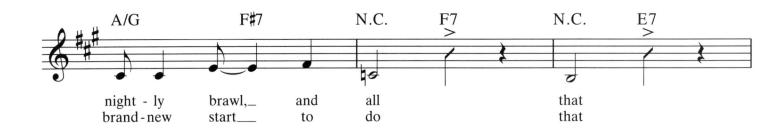

night - ly brawl,_ and all that
brand - new start___ to do that

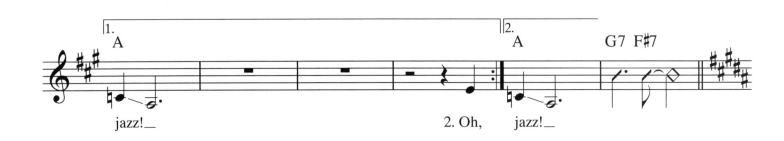

jazz!_   2. Oh,   jazz!_

A little faster ♩ = 126

Verse 3:

3.*(Oh,_____ you're gon - na see your She - ba shim - my shake,_)   oh, and

*Lyrics in parentheses indicate background vocals.

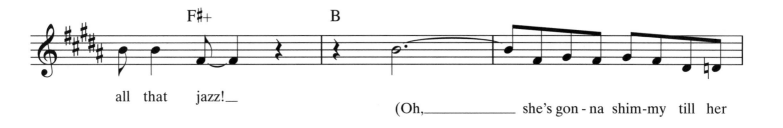

all that jazz!__ (Oh,_____ she's gon-na shim-my till her

gar-ters break,_) oh, and all that jazz!__ (Show_____

__ her where to park her gir-dle. Oh,_____ her moth-er's blood-'d cur-dle

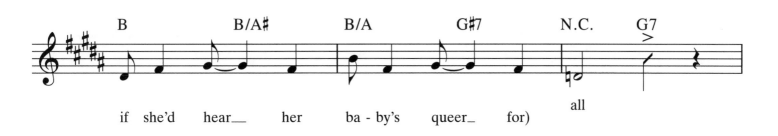

if she'd hear__ her ba-by's queer_ for) all

that jazz!_____

6

Verse 4:

4. Find a flask;_ we're play-in' fast and loose,_ and all that jazz!_ (And

all that jazz!_) Right up here_ is where I store the juice,_ and

all that jazz!_ (And all that jazz!_) Come on, babe,_ we're gon-na

brush the sky;___ I bet-cha Luck-y Lin-dy nev-er

flew so high._ 'Cause in the strat-o-sphere,_ how could he lend an ear_ to

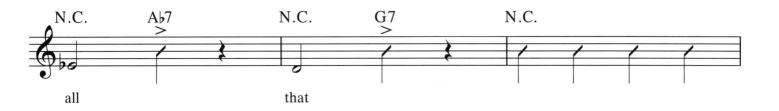

all   that

Spoken: (Fred: *Yeah, I'm afraid so, kiddo…*)

*jazz!*_____ *So that's final, huh, Fred?*   *Oh, Fred…*

(Fred: *Yeah?*)   F7

Nobody walks out on me!

Outro:

No,   I'm   no one's   wife,_   but   oh,   I   love my   life__   and

C7   *(Inst.)*   F7

all   that

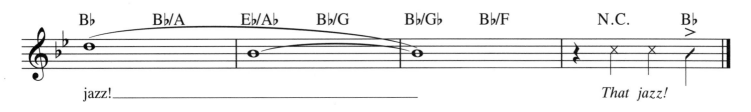

jazz!_____ *That jazz!*

Anything Goes

From *Anything Goes*
Words and Music by
COLE PORTER

Intro:
Times have changed,
and we've often rewound the clock
since the Puritans got a shock
when they landed on Plymouth Rock.
But today any shock
they should try to stem,
'stead of landing on Plymouth Rock,
Plymouth Rock would land on them.

Verse 1:
In olden days a glimpse of stocking
was looked on as something shocking,
but now God knows,
anything goes.
Good authors to who
once knew better words
now only use four-letter words
writing prose,
anything goes.
The world has gone mad today.
And good's bad today.
And black's white today.
And day's night today
and most guys today,
that women prize today,
are just silly gigolos.
So though I'm not a great romancer
I know that you're bound to answer
when I propose, anything goes.

Verse 2:
When Grandmama, whose age is eighty,
in nightclubs is getting matey
with gigolos,
anything goes.
When mothers pack and leave poor father
because they decide they'd rather
be tennis pros,
anything goes.
If driving fast cars you like,
or low bars you like,
or bare limbs you like,
or Mae West you like,
or me undressed you like,
to molest at night,
nobody will oppose.
When ev'ry night, the set that's smart
is indulging in nudist parties
in studios,
anything goes.

Outro:
*(Just think of those shocks you've got
and those knocks you've got
and those blues you've got
from that news you've got.
And those pains you've got,
if any brains you've got
from those little radios.)

They think he's gangster number one,
so they've made him the fav'rite son
and that goes to show
anything goes,
anything, anything, anything goes!

*Lyrics in parentheses indicate background vocals.

Anything Goes

From *Anything Goes*

Words and Music by
COLE PORTER

Moderately ♩ = 126

N.C. *Intro:*

Times have

changed,_____ and we've of - ten re - wound the clock__

since the Pu - ri - tans got a shock__ when they land - ed on

G7

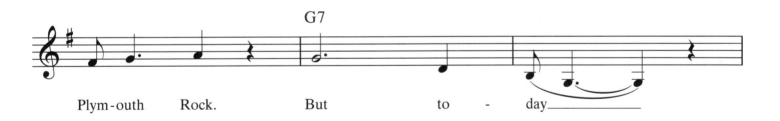

Plym - outh Rock. But to - day_____

Cm   D7

an - y shock they should try to stem,__ 'stead of land - ing on

Gm   *rall.*   D   A7   D7

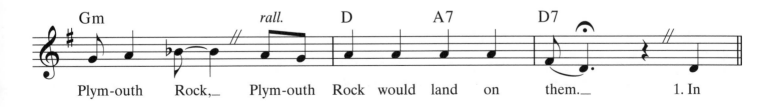

Plym - outh Rock,__ Plym - outh Rock would land on them.__ 1. In

Anything Goes - 5 - 1
26499

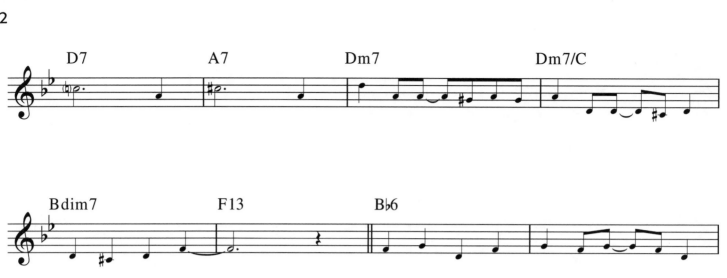

* (Just think_ of those

shocks you've got___ and those knocks you've got___ and those blues you've got___ from that

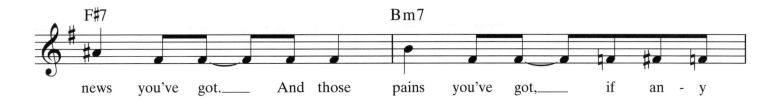

news you've got.___ And those pains you've got,___ if an - y

brains you've got___ from those lit - tle ra - di - os.___) They

think he's gang - ster num - ber one,___ so they've made him the fa - v'rite son___

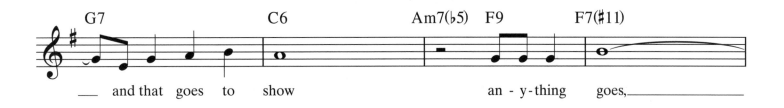

___ and that goes to show an - y-thing goes,_____

___ an - y-thing, an - y-thing, an - y - thing

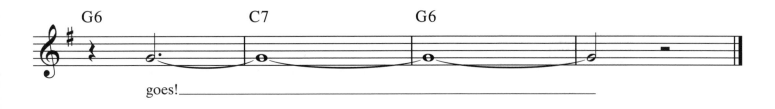

goes!_____

Aquarius

From *Hair*
Words by
JAMES RADO and GEROME RAGNI
Music by
GALT MacDERMOT

When the moon is in the seventh house,
and Jupiter aligns with Mars,
then peace will guide the planets,
and love will steer the stars.

This is the dawning of the age of Aquarius,
the age of Aquarius,
Aquarius, Aquarius.

Harmony and understanding.
Sympathy and trust abounding.
No more falsehoods or derisions,
golden living, dreams of visions,
mystic crystal revelations,
and the mind's true liberation,
Aquarius, Aquarius.

When the moon is in the seventh house,
and Jupiter aligns with Mars,
then peace will guide the planets,
and love will steer the stars.

This is the dawning of the age of Aquarius,
the age of Aquarius,
Aquarius, Aquarius.
Aquarius, Aquarius, Aquarius.

Aquarius

From *Hair*

Words by
JAMES RADO and
GEROME RAGNI

Music by
GALT MacDERMOT

Moderately bright rock ♩ = 84

N.C.

(Sound effects) *(Bass)*

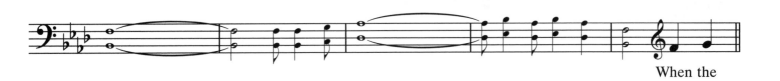

When the

moon_____ is in the sev-enth house,_____ and

Ju - pi - ter_____ a - ligns_ with_ Mars,_____ then

Aquarius - 3 - 1
26499

peace_____ will guide_ the plan - ets,_____ and

love_____ will steer the stars.__ This is the dawn - ing of the

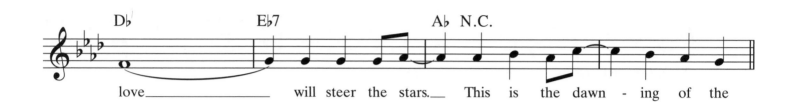

age of A - quar - i - us,___ the age of A - quar - i - us,_____

_____ A - quar - i - us,_____

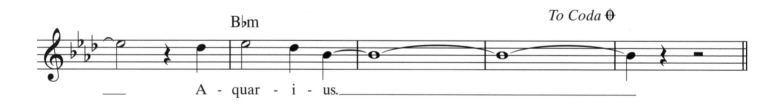

___ A - quar - i - us._____

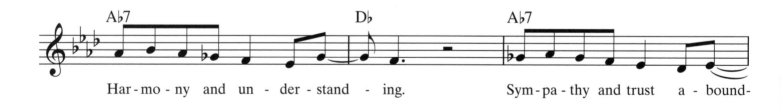

Har - mo - ny and un - der - stand - ing. Sym - pa - thy and trust a - bound-

ing.___ No more false-hoods or de - ri - sions, gold - en

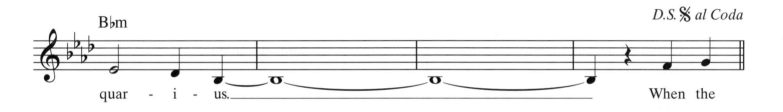

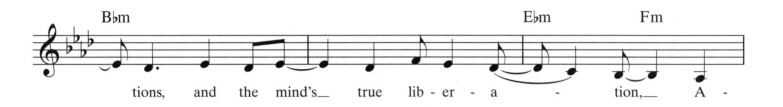

Dancing Queen

From *Mamma Mia!*

Words and Music by
BENNY ANDERSSON, STIG ANDERSON
and BJÖRN ULVAEUS

Ooh, you can dance,
you can jive,
having the time of your life.
Ooh, see that girl,
watch that scene,
diggin' the dancing queen.

Verse 1:
Friday night and the lights are low,
looking out for a place to go,
mm, where they play the right music,
getting in the swing.
You come to look for a king.

Verse 2:
Anybody can be that guy.
Night is young and the music's high.
With a bit of rock music,
ev'rything is fine.
You're in the mood for a dance.
And when you get the chance…

Chorus:
You are the dancing queen.
Young and sweet, only seventeen.
Dancing queen,
feel the beat from the tambourine.
You can dance, you can jive,
having the time of your life.
Ooh, see that girl, watch that scene,
diggin' the dancing queen.

Verse 3:
You're a teaser, you turn 'em on.
Leave 'em burnin' and then you're gone.
Lookin' out for another,
anyone will do.
You're in the mood for a dance.
And when you get the chance…

Chorus:
You are the dancing queen.
Young and sweet, only seventeen.
Dancing queen,
feel the beat from the tambourine.
You can dance, you can jive,
having the time of your life.
Ooh, see that girl, watch that scene,
diggin' the dancing queen.
Diggin' the dancing queen.

Dancing Queen

From Mamma Mia!

Words and Music by
BENNY ANDERSSON,
STIG ANDERSON and
BJÖRN ULVAEUS

Disco rock ♩ = 100

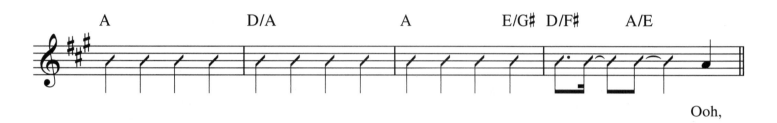

Ooh,

you can dance,__ you can jive,_____ hav - ing__ the time of__ your

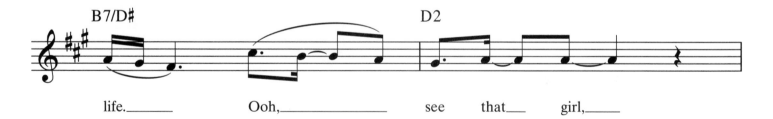

life._____ Ooh,_____ see that__ girl,_____

watch that_ scene, dig - gin' the danc - ing__ queen._____

Dancing Queen - 4 - 1
26493

Verse 1:

1. Fri - day night__ and the lights are low,_____

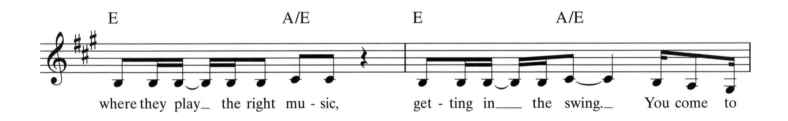

look - ing out___ for a place to go,_____ mm,___

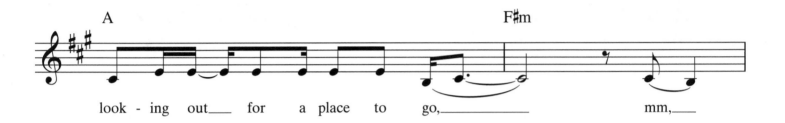

where they play__ the right mu - sic, get - ting in___ the swing.__ You come to

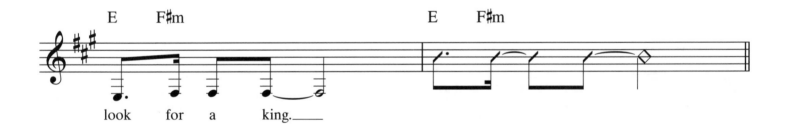

look for a king.____

Verses 2 & 3:

2. An - y - bod - y can be that guy._____
3. You're a teas - er, you turn 'em on._____

Night is young__ and the mu - sic's high._____
Leave 'em burn - in' and then you're gone._____

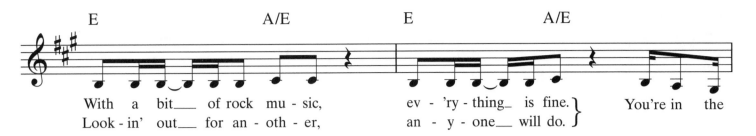

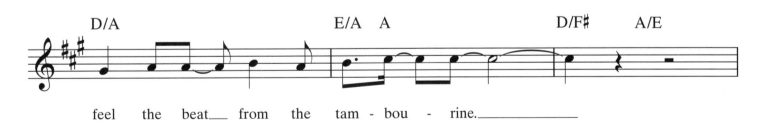

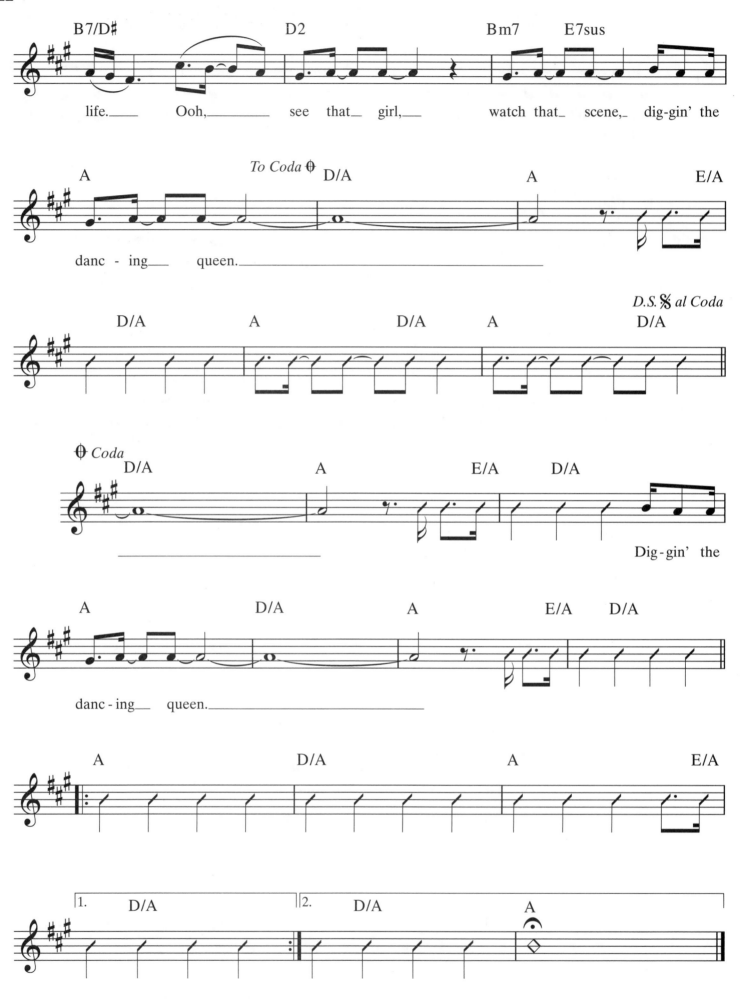

Diamonds Are a Girl's Best Friend

From *Gentlemen Prefer Blondes*
Words by
LEO ROBIN
Music by
JULE STYNE

Verse 1:
A kiss on the hand
may be quite Continental,
but diamonds are a girl's best friend.
A kiss may be grand,
but it won't pay the rental
on your humble flat
or help you at the Automat.
Men grow cold as girls grow old
and we all lose our charms in the end.
But square-cut or pear-shaped,
these rocks don't lose their shape,
diamonds are a girl's best friend.

Verse 2:
There may come a time
when a lass needs a lawyer,
but diamonds are a girl's best friend.
There may come a time
when a hard-boiled employer
thinks you're awful nice,
but get that "ice" or else no dice.
He's your guy when stocks are high,
but beware when they start to descend.
It's then that those louses
go back to their spouses,
diamonds are a girl's best friend.

Verse 3:
I've heard of affairs
that are strictly platonic,
but diamonds are a girl's best friend.
And I think affairs
that that you must keep liaisonic
are better bets
if little pets get big baguettes.
Time rolls on and youth is gone
and you can't straighten up when you bend.
But stiff back or stiff knees,
you stand straight at Tiff'ny's,
diamonds are a girl's best friend.

Diamonds Are a Girl's Best Friend

From *Gentlemen Prefer Blondes*

Words by
LEO ROBIN

Music by
JULE STYNE

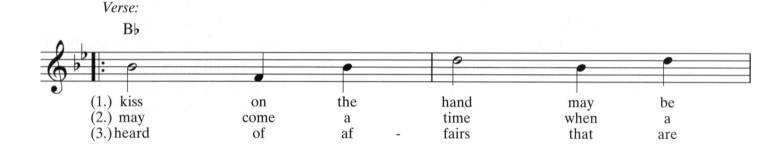

Verse:

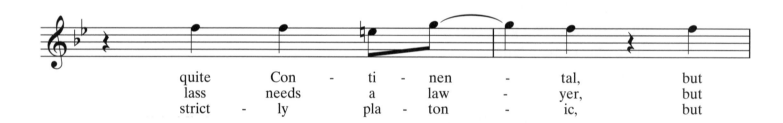

(1.) kiss on the hand may be
(2.) may come a time when a
(3.) heard of af - fairs that are

quite Con - ti - nen - tal, but
lass needs a law - yer, but
strict - ly pla - ton - ic, but

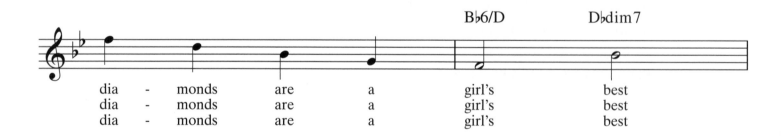

dia - monds are a girl's best
dia - monds are a girl's best
dia - monds are a girl's best

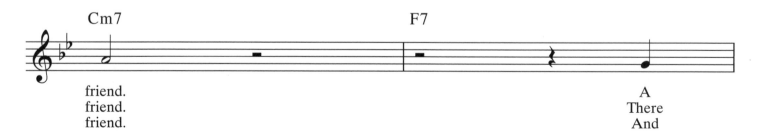

friend.
friend.
friend.

A
There
And

Diamonds Are a Girl's Best Friend - 3 - 1
26499

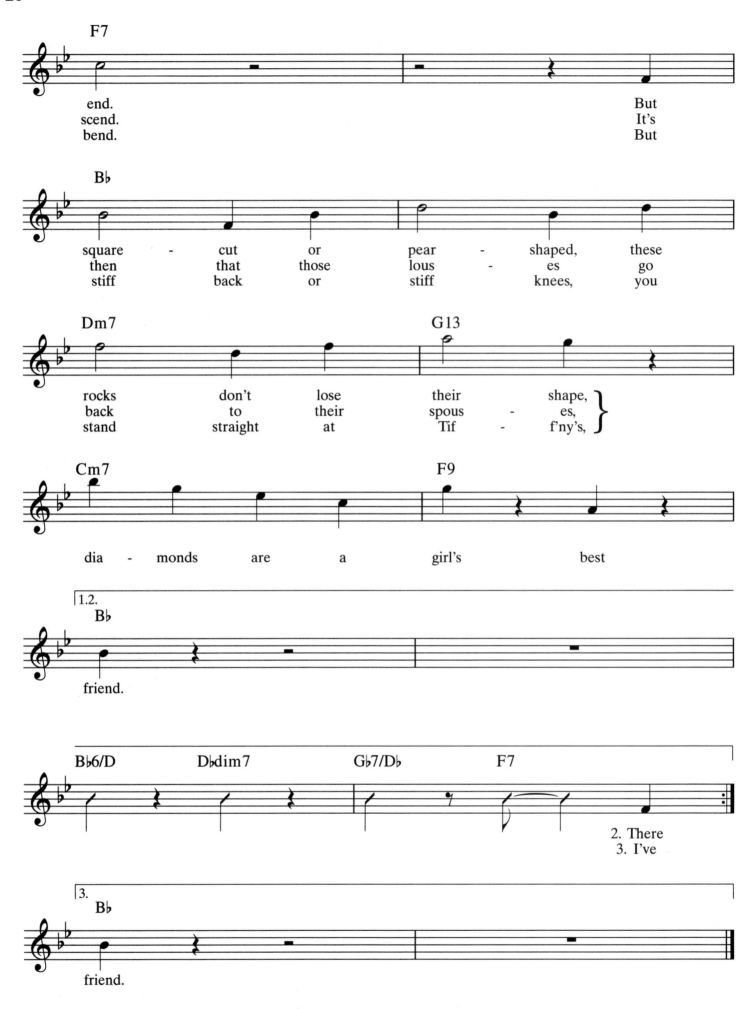

How Could I Ever Know?

From *The Secret Garden*
Words and Music by
MARSHA NORMAN and LUCY SIMON

How could I know I would have to leave you?
How could I know I would hurt you so?
You were the one I was born to love,
oh, how could I ever know?
How could I ever know?

How can I say to go on without me?
How, when I know you still need me so?
How can I say not to dream about me?
How could I ever know?
How could I ever know?

Forgive me, can you forgive me,
and hold me in your heart?
And find some new way to love me,
now that we're apart?

How could I know I would never hold you?
Never again in this world,
but oh, sure as you breathe,
I am there inside you.
How could I ever know?
How could I ever know?

Archibald:
How can I hope to go on without you?
How can I know where you'd have me go?
How can I bear not to dream about you?
How can I let you go?
Lily:
How could I ever know?
Archibald:
All I need is…
Lily:
…is there in the garden.
Archibald:
All I would ask is…
Lily:
…is care for the child of
Both:
our love.
Lily:
Come go with me:
Safe I will keep you.
Archibald:
Where would you lead me,
there I would…
Lily:
There I would, there we would,
Both:
there we will go.
How, how could I know?
Tell me, how, how could I know?
Ever to know you will never leave me.
How,
Archibald:
could we ever know?
Lily:
how could we know?
Both:
How could I ever know?

How Could I Ever Know?

From *The Secret Garden*

Words and Music by
MARSHA NORMAN
and LUCY SIMON

Slowly and gently ♩ = 69

How__ could I know I would have to leave you?

How__ could I know I would hurt you so? You__ were the one I was

born to love, oh, how_____ could I ev - er know?

Andante con moto *(non rubato)* ♩ = 76

How_____ could I ev - er know?_____

How__ can I say to go on with-out me? How,__ when I know you still

need me so? How__ can I say not to dream a - bout me?

How could I ev - er know? How_____ could I ev - er

Poco più mosso, *more freely*

know? For - give me, can you for - give me, and

hold me in your heart? And find some new way to

love me, now that we're a - part? _____

Meno mosso

How__ could I know I would nev - er hold you? Nev - er a - gain in this

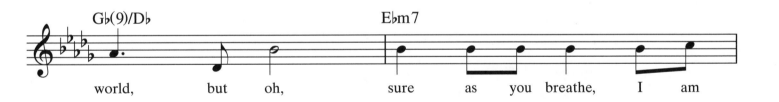

world, but oh, sure as you breathe, I am

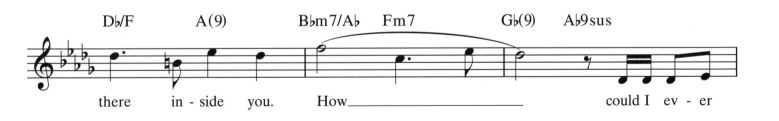

there in - side you. How_____ could I ev - er

know? _____ How_____ could I ev - er

30

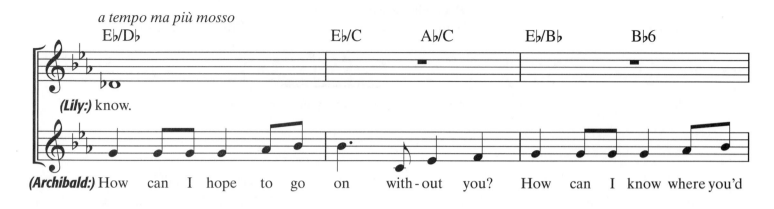

a tempo ma più mosso

Eb/Db   Eb/C   Ab/C   Eb/Bb   Bb6

(Lily:) know.

(Archibald:) How can I hope to go on with-out you? How can I know where you'd

Absus   Ab   Fm7   Eb(9)/G   B(9)

have me go? How can I bear not to dream a-bout you?

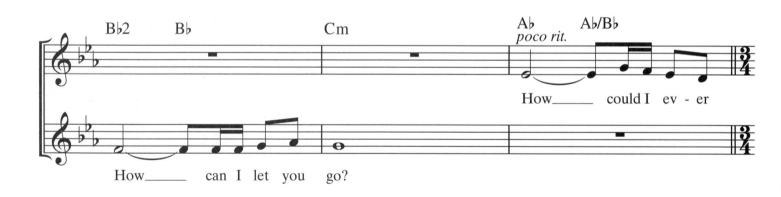

Bb2   Bb   Cm   Ab   Ab/Bb
                                                     poco rit.

How___ can I let you go?

                                             How___ could I ev-er

Eb(9)   Bb6   Cm(9)
a tempo ♩=♩.   *3*

know?_____   ...is___ there_ in the gar - den.___

All I need is...___

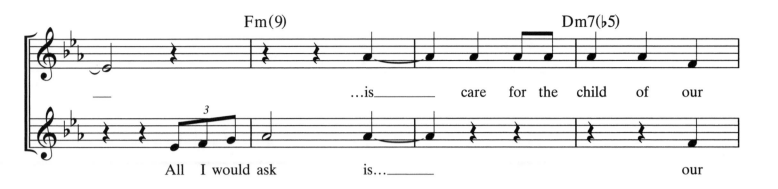

How Could I Ever Know? - 5 - 4
26499

32

Molto passionato

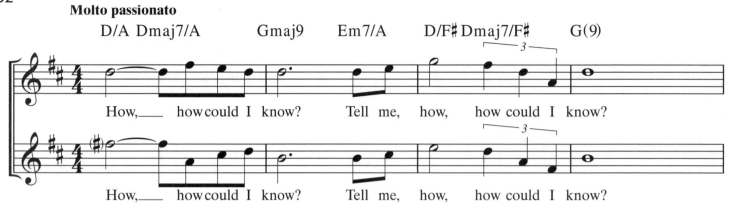

How,___ how could I know? Tell me, how, how could I know?

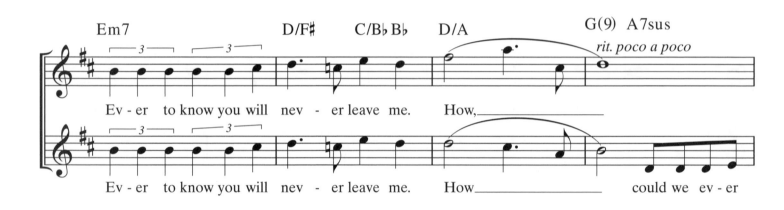

Ev - er to know you will nev - er leave me. How,___

Ev - er to know you will nev - er leave me. How___ could we ev - er

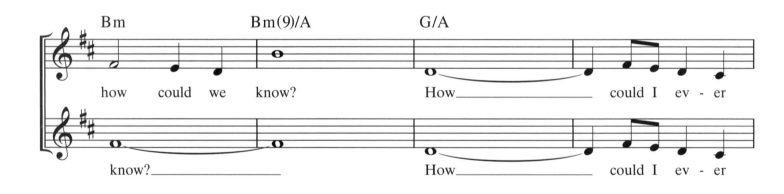

how could we know? How___ could I ev - er

know?___ How___ could I ev - er

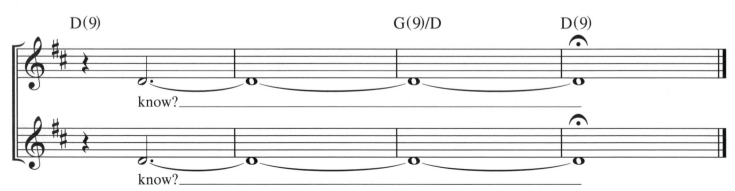

know?___

know?___

How Could I Ever Know? - 5 - 5
26499

Send in the Clowns

From *A Little Night Music*
Music and Lyrics by
STEPHEN SONDHEIM

Isn't it rich?
Are we a pair?
Me here at last on the ground,
you in midair…
Where are the clowns?

Isn't it bliss?
Don't you approve?
One who keeps tearing around,
one who can't move…
Where are the clowns?
Send in the clowns.

Just when I'd stopped
opening doors,
finally knowing the one that I
wanted was yours,
making my entrance again
with my usual flair,
sure of my lines, no one is there.

Don't you love farce?
My fault, I fear.
I thought that you'd want what I want.
Sorry, my dear.
But where are the clowns?
Quick, send in the clowns.
Don't bother, they're here.

Isn't it rich,
isn't it queer,
losing my timing this late
in my career?
And where are the clowns?
There ought to be clowns?
Well, maybe next year…

Send in the Clowns

From *A Little Night Music*

Music and Lyrics by
STEPHEN SONDHEIM

Slowly, freely ♩. = 60

N.C.

(Oboe)

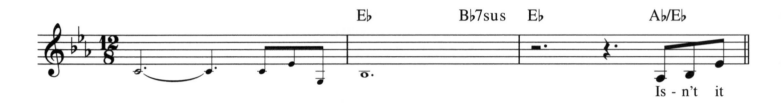

Is - n't it

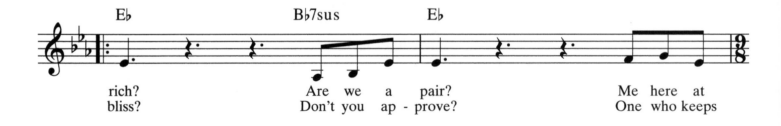

rich?
bliss?

Are we a pair?
Don't you ap - prove?

Me here at
One who keeps

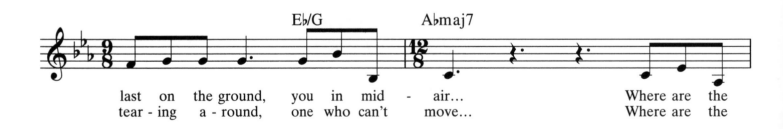

last on the ground,
tear - ing a - round,

you in mid - air...
one who can't move...

Where are the
Where are the

clowns?

Is - n't it

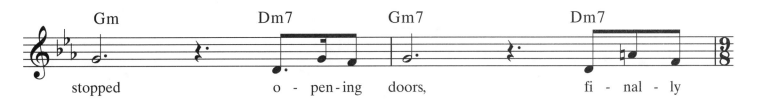

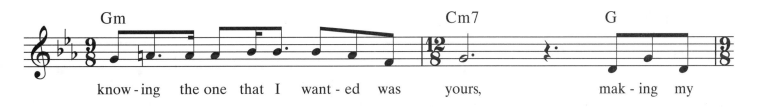

36

farce? My fault, I fear. I thought that
rich, is - n't it queer, los - ing my

you'd want what I want. Sor - ry, my dear. But where are the
tim - ing this late in my ca - reer? And where are the

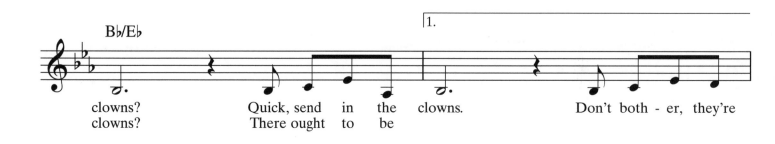

1.
clowns? Quick, send in the clowns. Don't both - er, they're
clowns? There ought to be

2.
here. Is - n't it clowns. Well, may - be next

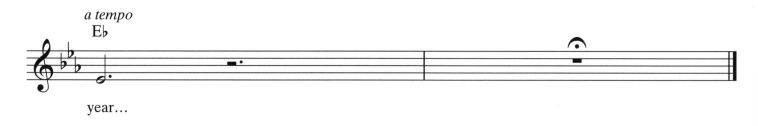

a tempo

year...

Send in the Clowns - 3 - 3
26499

Whatever Lola Wants (Lola Gets)

From *Damn Yankees*
Words and Music by
RICHARD ADLER and JERRY ROSS

Whatever Lola wants,
Lola gets,
and, little man,
little Lola wants you.
Make up your mind
to have no regrets.
Recline yourself,
resign yourself,
you're through.

I always get
what I aim for,
and your heart and soul
is what I came for.

Whatever Lola wants,
Lola gets.
Take off your coat,
don't you know you can't win?
You're no exception to the rule;
I'm irresistible, you fool, give in.
Whatever Lola wants,
Lola gets.

I always get
what I aim for,
and your heart and soul
is what I came for.

Whatever Lola wants,
Lola gets.
Take off your coat,
don't you know you can't win?
You're no exception to the rule;
I'm irresistible, you fool,
give in,
give in,
give in.

Whatever Lola Wants (Lola Gets)

From *Damn Yankees*

Words and Music by
RICHARD ADLER
and JERRY ROSS